MW01671537

Great Strides

Literal Skills

Rigby®
A Harcourt Achieve Imprint

www.Rigby.com
1-800-531-5015

ACKNOWLEDGMENTS

STAFF CREDITS
Editorial: Vicky Aeschbacher, Heera Kang, Lori Najar, Tina Posner
Design: Amy Braden, Joan Cunningham, Joyce Spicer

PHOTOGRAPHY
P. 8 ©Coneyl Jay/Photo Researchers, Inc; p. 9 ©Spencer Grant/Photo Researchers, Inc; p. 15 ©NASA; p. 20 ©Kin Cheung/Reuters/CORBIS; p. 26 ©VIEW Pictures Ltd./Alamy; p. 27 ©Jo Hale/Getty Images; p. 30 ©Gary Bell/oceanwideimages.com; p. 31 ©Gary Bell/oceanwideimages.com; p. 36 ©Scott Barbour/Getty Images; p. 37 ©George Rodger/Time Life Pictures/Getty Images; p. 42 ©United States Patent and Trademark Office; p. 43 ©United States Patent and Trademark Office; p. 46 ©AFP/Getty Images; p. 47 ©AP Photo/Rob Griffith; p. 58 ©David Cohen.

Additional photography by Getty Images Royalty Free, Photos.com Royalty Free, PhotoDisc/Getty Images and Royalty-Free/CORBIS.

ISBN 1-4189-2910-7

Printed in the United States of America

1 2 3 4 5 6 7 8 9 059 10 09 08 07 06 05

Literal Skills help you find stated information.

So you will be able to:

- use different parts of a book, such as a glossary or an index.
- look for facts and details stated in sentences or chapters.
- learn how to use text features, such as charts, maps, or timelines.

Table of Contents

Literal Skills Roleplay

Student 1:	The question asks us about the stages in the life cycle of a butterfly.
Student 2:	Maybe our science book has the information we need.
Student 3:	OK. I'm looking in the Table of Contents.
Student 1:	I see it. It should be in Chapter 3.
Student 3:	Yeah, I looked in the index, too. Try page 72.
Student 3:	That's right. Here it is.
Teacher:	Good job finding the right part of the book. Now, how will you use the information on that page to answer the question?
Student 1:	We need to put the information into the right order.
Student 3:	This diagram shows each step in the process.
Student 3:	The headings help, too. They give a little more information about each step.
Teacher:	Great work. When you are looking for information that can be found right in a text, you are using literal skills.

Your Turn

Read the list of tasks. Then sort them into the chart below. Remember, when you use literal skills, you're looking for specific information on the page.

- Looking for a fact or a group of facts
- Using your experience to figure out how a character feels
- Using a timeline to see when an event happened
- Predicting the next president of the United States
- Deciding if school uniforms are a good idea
- Looking for information on a chart or map

Literal Skills Are Good For	Literal Skills Are NOT Good For

Write Back...

Next time you're looking for information that is stated on the page, what will you do?

ROBOTS Save Lives

Robots to the rescue!

Comprehension Skills

- **Lesson 2:** Using Text Features: Titles and Sidebars
- **Lesson 3:** Using Text Features: Images and Captions

Reading Strategy

Adjust Your Reading Rate

Change your reading speed depending on your purpose for reading. You may need to concentrate on every word to remember what you read. You may need to read quickly for information.

Would you want to walk up to a bomb? Someone has to get close and take the bomb apart so it won't explode. Most people wouldn't want to do that job. So it is a good job for robots. After all, robots won't be afraid. A robot just might save human lives.

Robots Find Bombs

When there is a bomb scare, it is important to find the bomb before it goes off. That can be hard. Many bombs are small. They are often hidden. The Mini-ANDROS robot can find and **disable** bombs. It has two arms. It can move around in small spaces. It can even climb stairs. The Mini-ANDROS is a member of many bomb teams today. It has saved many human lives.

Landmines are bombs that people put underground during war. After the war, landmines are still there. When someone steps on the ground near a landmine, the bomb can explode. It's a big problem. The STAR robot

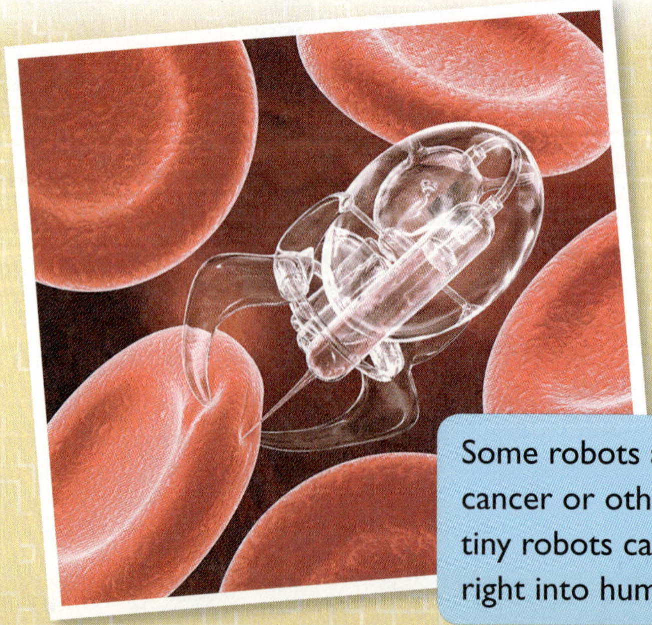

Some robots are used to fight cancer or other diseases. These tiny robots can inject medicine right into human blood cells.

This robot has a long arm to pick up bombs. It can destroy the bombs, take photographs, and even open doors to find bombs.

was built to disable landmines. The robot is connected to a computer with a video camera. The computer tells the robot how to disable the landmine. Once the landmine is disabled, it will not go off.

Robots in Disasters

After an earthquake, rescue teams search for survivors. People just might be caught under **rubble**. Rescue teams use the TerminatorBot to help. The TerminatorBot is about 3 inches around and 8 inches long. It has two front legs to help it crawl. It can crawl through small openings in rubble to search for survivors. When it finds people who are trapped, it can inform rescue teams. Then, the rescue teams can move in to help people get out.

The Future of Life-Saving Robots

Robots keep getting smarter and easier to use. In the future, robots will probably be used to save even more human lives. ■

No Sick Robots

Sometimes robots are used for everyday work in factories or power plants. They can work with dangerous chemicals that would make people sick. Robug III is one of these robots. It works in nuclear plants. It can step over large **obstacles**.

Vocabulary

disable: make something so it can't work anymore
rubble: material (such as bricks) that has fallen after a building is destroyed
obstacles: things in the way

Lesson 2

Using Text Features: Titles and Sidebars

Your Turn

Reread the title, the headings in the text, and the heading for the sidebar. Then, fill in each box below.

The title tells me that this passage is about

The section with the heading Robots Find Bombs is about

The section with the heading Robots in Disasters is about

The sidebar is about

Your Choice

Circle the correct answer.

1. **According to the article, robots can —**

   A. work in restaurants.
   B. climb mountain sides.
   C. work as soldiers.
   D. find disaster survivors.

2. **In which section can you read about Robug III?**

   A. Robots Find Bombs
   B. The Future of Life-Saving Robots
   C. No Sick Robots
   D. Robots in Disasters

3. **Robots in Disasters tells about the —**

   A. Mini-ANDROS.
   B. STAR robot.
   C. Robug III.
   D. TerminatorBot.

4. **To disable something, you might have to —**

   A. turn it around.
   B. take it apart.
   C. fix it.
   D. build it.

(See answers for Literal Skills, Lesson 2 to check your work.)

Number Correct:

Write Back...

How can using text features help you find information quickly?

Lesson 3

Using Text Features: Images and Captions

Your Turn

Read "Robots Save Lives" again. Look at the images (pictures), and read the captions (the words below the pictures). Then, fill in each box below.

The image from page 8 shows	Its caption tells about

The image from page 9 shows	Its caption tells about

Your Choice

Circle the correct answer.

1. **Which robot is used to find earthquake survivors?**

   A. TerminatorBot
   B. Robug III
   C. STAR robot
   D. Mini-ANDROS

2. **From reading the captions, you can see that some robots save lives by —**

   A. killing insects.
   B. rescuing people.
   C. fighting diseases.
   D. fighting wars.

3. **From looking at the picture on page 9 you can see that some robots —**

   A. have long arms or claws.
   B. look like humans.
   C. have legs to climb stairs.
   D. are too tiny to see.

4. **Why would it be useful for robots to step over obstacles?**

   A. obstacles help them find bombs.
   B. obstacles get in the way.
   C. obstacles disable robots.
   D. obstacles always blow up.

(See answers for Literal Skills, Lesson 3 to check your work.)

Number Correct:

Write Back...

How does looking at images and captions help you?

Sputnik

Comprehension Skills

- **Lesson 4:** Scanning for Keywords
- **Lesson 5:** Using Parts of a Book

Reading Strategy

Question Yourself
Ask yourself questions about what you are reading. How do satellites help cell phone users? What was the very first human-made satellite? Write notes in the margin.

Sputnik's Claim to Fame

Do you know how your cell phone really works?

Your cell phone is ringing! A **satellite** helped send that call. At the same moment, the satellite sent more than one thousand other calls all over the world. When your cell phone rang, so did at least one thousand other cell phones.

Satellites, Natural or Human-Made

A satellite is an object in space. It orbits a larger object. Here is an example. The moon follows a path in space around Earth. The Moon is a natural satellite. Today, over 8,000 human-made satellites circle Earth too.

Sputnik, the Start of the Call

In 1957, the Soviets sent a satellite into space. It was called *Sputnik 1*. It was the start of the space race. The United States was going head-to-head with The Soviet Union. Who would be the first to get to the moon? Scientists would run this race. Technology would win it. The space race brought change. After *Sputnik*, students in the United States studied more science and math. This was part of a plan to develop the space program.

Space Exploration

INDEX

GLOSSARY

astronaut: a person who travels to space
data: facts; information
International Space Station: the world's largest satellite
launch: the start or beginning of something
orbit: (*noun*) the path taken by one body circling another body. *The Earth follows an orbit around the sun.*
orbit: (*verb*) to move in an orbit around; to circle. *The moon orbits our planet.*

The International Space Station took years to build.

A New View of Earth

Satellites can collect and send information. The first satellites sent back pictures of Earth. No one had seen anything like this before. Suddenly, people could see what Earth looked like. From way out in space, they could finally get the big picture. They could see hurricanes forming. They could see plumes of smoke rising from volcanoes. They could track ships at sea.

International Space Station

Sputnik 1 looked like a silver beach ball. It was two feet across and weighed 184 pounds. Today, the largest human-made satellite weighs much more. It is the International Space Station. When it is finished, it will weigh almost one million pounds. Astronauts from Russia and the United States are working together to **assemble** it. It is taking years to build. It is another sort of space race. One the United States and Russia are winning together.

How Does It Stay in Orbit?

How do you keep a big satellite in orbit? You have to send it up very high. The International Space Station is 235 miles above the planet. Here is the odd part. It is always falling toward Earth. No need to worry though. Luckily, there are laws of science that keep things right where they should be. Now that's another story. ■

Vocabulary

satellite: a natural or human-made object in space that circles another object
assemble: to fit or join together

Scanning for Keywords

Your Turn

Scan "Sputnik's Claim to Fame". Underline keywords, words that are important to the topic. Then, write them into the web below.

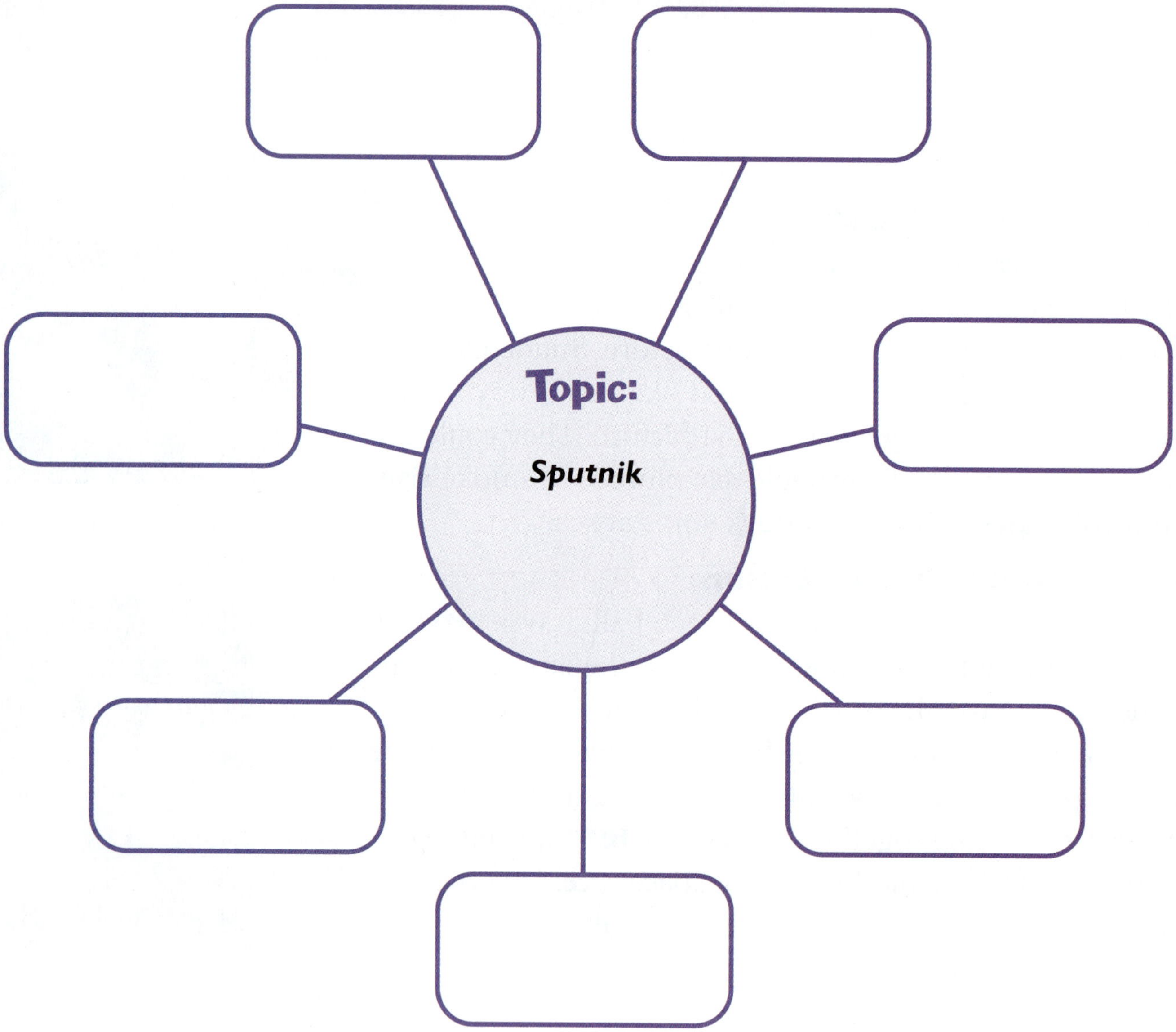

Your Choice

Circle the correct answer.

1 ***Sputnik I* was —**

A. the size of a 5-bedroom house.
B. the start of the space race.
C. on the moon.
D. put into orbit by the United States.

2 **Which keyword is the most important in this article?**

A. satellite
B. planet
C. human
D. orbit

3 **Which keyword tells what kind of satellite *Sputnik* is?**

A. orbit.
B. human-made.
C. planet.
D. Earth.

4 **Which item would a buyer most likely have to assemble?**

A. a car
B. a photo album
C. a desk
D. a book

(See answers for Literal Skills, Lesson 4 to check your work.)

Number Correct:

Write Back...

What did you learn about keywords that can help you understand the important information in the text?

Lesson 5

Using Parts of a Book

Your Turn

Use the index and glossary on pages 14–15 and the *Great Strides* Table of Contents to answer the questions below.

	Table of Contents	Glossary	Index
Where can you find the meaning of the word *launch*?			
Where can you find page numbers for more information about communication with satellites?			
What is organized in alphabetical order?			
Where can you go to find the page numbers for "Two World Records in One Balloon"?			

Your Choice

Circle the correct answer.

1. **Satellites help people by —**

   A. collecting information about hurricanes and volcanoes.
   B. always falling toward Earth.
   C. studying math and science so people don't have to.
   D. developing the space program.

2. **The index tells you —**

   A. where you can find the titles of other books.
   B. where to find information on certain topics.
   C. where to find the captions for photographs.
   D. the definition of new words.

3. **If you look up *orbit* in the glossary, you will find —**

   A. a list of pages about orbits.
   B. the meaning of *orbit*.
   C. questions to answer about orbits.
   D. how to put a satellite into orbit.

4. **Which of the following is a satellite?**

   A. the moon
   B. a cell phone
   C. a rocket
   D. an orbit

(See answers for Literal Skills, Lesson 5 to check your work.)

Number Correct:

Write Back...

If you wanted to learn more about how satellites stay in orbit, how would an index help you? What other ways can you use an index?

Rescue on the Beach

Find out how elephants became heroes.

Comprehension Skills

- **Lesson 6:** Reading a Map
- **Lesson 7:** Understanding Directions

Reading Strategy

Picture in Your Mind
Try to picture what you read. Turn the words into a movie in your mind. See what is happening.

Have you ever heard an elephant cry? It sounds like a trumpet, only much louder. On December 26, 2004, the people of Khao Lak (kau' lak'), Thailand heard that sound. Something was very wrong. The elephants had never cried like that before.

Elephants are common in Khao Lak. People ride them along the beaches. On this morning, no one could quiet the elephants. Without warning, the elephants raced toward higher ground.

The people soon saw why the elephants were running. A huge wave called a tsunami was roaring toward them. The people began to run. The wave was about to hit the beach when an amazing thing happened. The elephants lifted some of the struggling people up a hill.

Khao Lak Beach is on the west corner of Thailand. It was hit by a giant wave in December 2004. You'll never guess who came to the rescue!

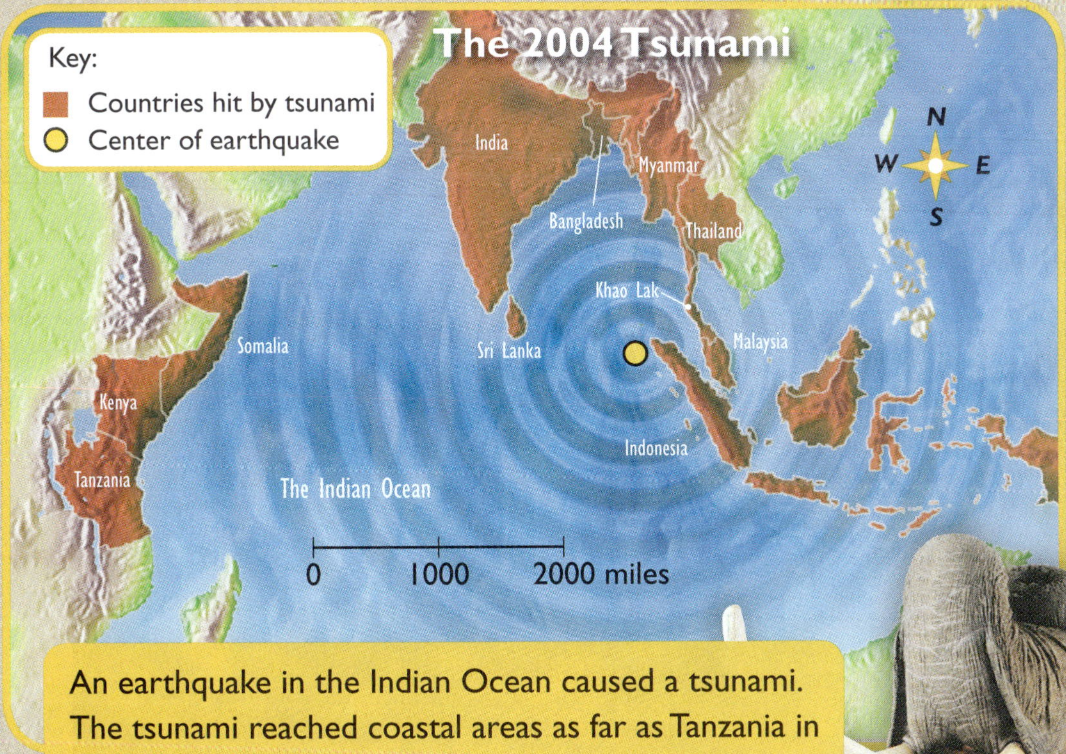

An earthquake in the Indian Ocean caused a tsunami. The tsunami reached coastal areas as far as Tanzania in Africa. Check out the scale of miles. Tanzania is about 4,000 miles away from the center of the earthquake!

The elephants rescued some people, but the raging tsunami drowned many others. The **coastal** areas were completely destroyed. Those people on that hilltop above Khao Lak Beach survived though, thanks to the elephants.

How did the elephants know the tsunami was coming? Did the elephants feel an earthquake? Did they see the ocean water **retreat** from the beach? Did they hear a loud sound like a roaring train? These are all tsunami warning signs. If you are ever in a coastal area and notice these signs, don't wait for elephants. Head for higher ground. Then, listen and respond to emergency messages. Finally, stay away from dangerous areas until the emergency has ended.

Perhaps the elephants recognized nature's warning signs. This is still a mystery. What we do know is that the elephants were heroes that day. ■

Vocabulary

coastal: near the sea
retreat: to move back away

Lesson

6 Reading a Map

Your Turn

Use this map to answer the questions below.

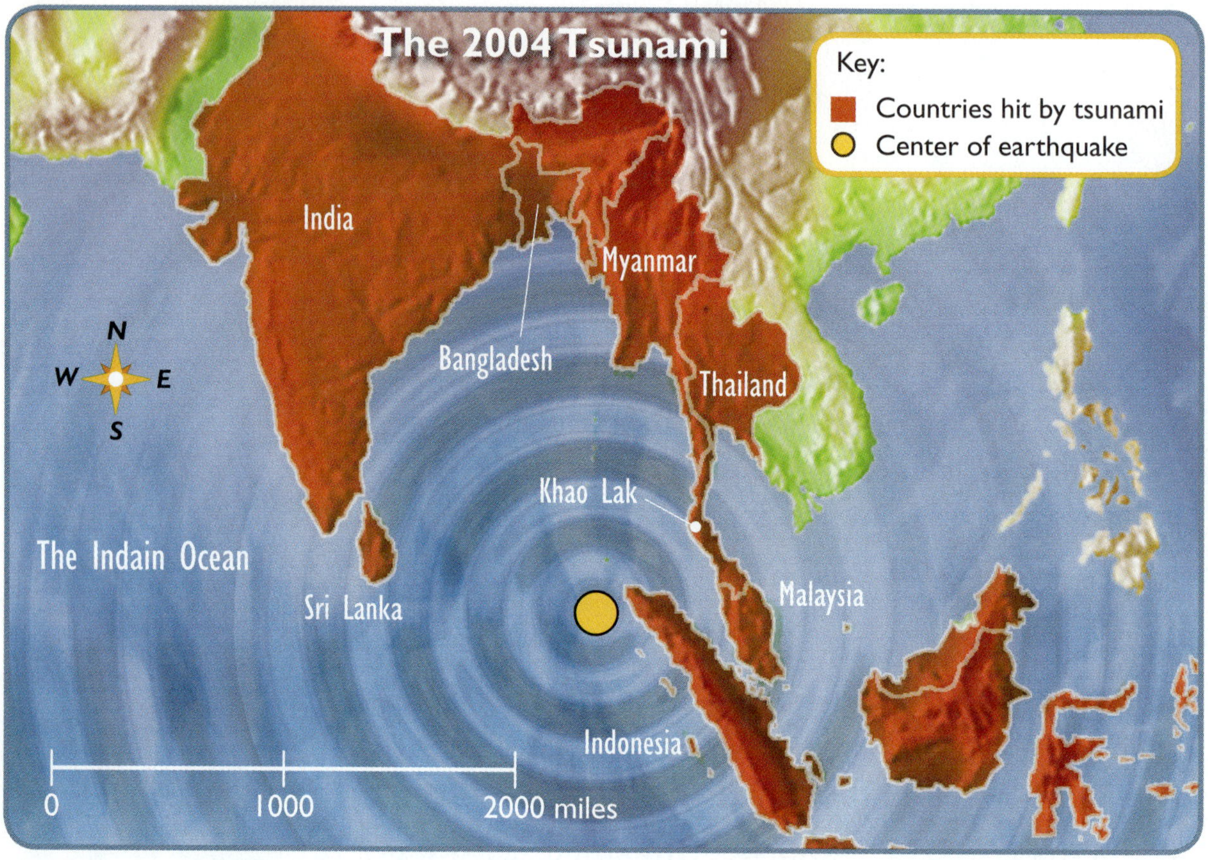

What is the country next to Thailand on the west?

What does the red area show on the map?

According to the scale, about how many miles was the earthquake from Khao Lak?

Your Choice

Circle the correct answer.

1 **Some people were able to survive the tsunami because the elephants —**

A. knew how far to run.
B. carried the people to safety.
C. warned them to run away.
D. were tame.

2 **On the map, how can you tell which countries were hit by the tsunami?**

A. their borders
B. their color
C. their names
D. the scale

3 **On a map, what does a compass rose tell you?**

A. population
B. rainfall
C. direction
D. distance

4 **The elephants retreated from the beach because they —**

A. wanted to get to higher ground.
B. wanted to give people a ride.
C. were following the people.
D. didn't like to get wet.

(See answers for Literal Skills, Lesson 6 to check your work.)

Number Correct:

Write Back...

What did you learn from using this map that you didn't know before?

Lesson 7

Understanding Directions

Your Turn

Reread the passage. As you read, write a number beside each step for what to do during a tsunami. Then, write the steps in order below.

How to Survive a Tsunami

Step 1

Step 2

Step 3

Step 4

Your Choice

Circle the correct answer.

1. **The elephants helped people up the hill because —**

   A. the people were in the way.
   B. a giant wave was coming.
   C. the people were wet.
   D. the elephants wanted to race.

2. **During a natural disaster, understanding directions can help you —**

   A. get ready for a disaster.
   B. know what to pack in a hurry.
   C. get through the disaster alive.
   D. know why disasters happen.

3. **What is the most important direction to follow in case of a tsunami?**

   A. Head for higher ground.
   B. Pack up your stuff.
   C. Follow the elephants.
   D. Climb a tree and watch the wave.

4. **Where is the worst place to be during a tsunami?**

   A. a mountain
   B. a city
   C. a coastal area
   D. an inland area

(See answers for Literal Skills, Lesson 7 to check your work.)

Number Correct:

Write Back...

What did you learn about understanding directions? How can this information help you?

STAGE EFFECTS
Fog and Mirrors

How do stage effects turn dull stages into dazzling concerts?

Comprehension Skills

You Have Already Learned

- Using Text Features: Titles and Sidebars
- Using Text Features: Images and Captions
- Scanning for Keywords
- Using Parts of a Book
- Reading a Map
- Understanding Directions

Screaming teens fill the stadium. A waterfall flows up from the crowd. Fog pours over the stage. Then the band appears out of thin air. Tears stream from a teenager's eyes. As she jumps up and down, she yells, "I can't believe this is really happening!"

The girl's actions are easy to understand. Companies work years to create exciting stage effects. And the girl's words are exactly what they want to hear. Stage effects companies want you to believe that the activity on stage is real.

Light and Mirror Tricks

Stage effects companies, such as Buenos Aires Laser, use projectors, lights, and mirrors to trick your eyes. Their projectors can send moving images across a stadium. One second you see a dancer on stage. The next second the dancer is on every wall. A second later he disappears.

Before the stage tricks begin, music halls look pretty dull.

Projectors, lights, and fog machines make concerts come alive.

FUN FACTS

Types of Stage Effects

Effects with Lights
- beams
- projected images

Effects with Chemicals
- fog
- snow
- smoke

Effects with Fire
- flames
- fireworks

How do they do it? First, an artist creates an image on a computer. Then, the projector sends the image to the stage. Finally, mirrors direct the image around the room.

Water and Light Tricks

The Laser Magic Company has another trick. Their stage waterfall flows up–not down. Does it really? Actually, drops of water fall from above. As they fall, a special lamp flashes tiny lights on the water. The lights move so quickly that your eyes are **deceived** into thinking that the water is moving upwards.

Chemical Tricks

Light isn't everything, though. Strictly FX uses a **chemical** to create stage fog. Their fog machine heats the chemical to make a gas. Then it frees the gas into the air. As the gas comes out, it looks like fog.

These tricks are great to see. But don't be fooled. Not everything you see on stage is "really happening." ■

Vocabulary

deceived: tricked

chemical: a substance that can combine or react with another

Lesson 8

Review

Your Turn

Use the Skills List to fill in the chart below. Then, decide if the skill is helpful with what you are reading. Explain why or why not.

Skills List

- reading a map
- scanning for keywords
- using parts of a book
- understanding directions
- using text features: titles and sidebars
- using text features: images and captions

Skill	Is Using This Skill Helpful with This Passage?
When you read the title, headings, and sidebars of a passage to get an idea about the topic, you could be ______	☐ Yes Why? ☐ No Why not?
When you use a scale to find the distance between two places, you could be ______	☐ Yes Why? ☐ No Why not?
When you look quickly through a text for the important words, you could be ______	☐ Yes Why? ☐ No Why not?
When you look for the definition of a word in a glossary, you could be ______	☐ Yes Why? ☐ No Why not?

Your Choice

Circle the correct answer.

1. To create fog, one company uses —

A. lasers and projectors.
B. lights and mirrors.
C. a chemical and heat
D. water and mirrors.

2. Which skill will help you quickly find information about tricks using flashing lights?

A. reading a map
B. using text features: titles and sidebars
C. understanding directions
D. using text features: images and captions

3. Which skill would be most useful if you wanted to learn how to make a stage effect?

A. reading a map of brazil
B. using the glossary in a social studies book
C. scanning for keywords in a newspaper article
D. understanding directions in an instruction manual

4. If someone has deceived you, that person has —

A. entertained you.
B. hurt you.
C. fooled you.
D. surprised you.

(See answers for Literal Skills, Lesson 8 to check your work.)

Number Correct:

Write Back...

How can literal skills help you find information when you read?

World's OLDEST LIVING CREATURE

Imagine being more than 170 years old!

Comprehension Skills

- **Lesson 9:** Sequencing with Signal Words
- **Lesson 10:** Reading a Chart

Reading Strategy

Reread
To understand the text better, read it a second time.

Imagine a birthday cake with over 170 candles on it. A giant tortoise named Harriet would probably want something a little different. But what? First, Harriet might enjoy a huge salad made of bean, eggplant, and squash. Next, hibiscus flowers for dessert would be nice. Then, a gentle scratch on her shell and under her legs would feel good. Finally, Harriet could spend the rest of the day napping in the pond. That would be Harriet's idea of a good time, and she's earned it.

Harriet was born in 1830 on the Galapogos Islands, off Ecuador in the Pacific Ocean. A scientist named Charles Darwin found her. He was exploring the islands in 1835. Back then, Harriet was only the size of a dinner plate. Darwin took her back to England to **examine** her. This was the first contact she had with people, but it wasn't her last.

Later, some sailors took her all the way to Australia. Then, they put her in a zoo. Many people visited her there. They didn't understand her very well, though. They called her Harry. Then they introduced "Harry" to other females, hoping that they would have babies. Of course, that didn't work! Finally, about 100 years later people realized that Harry was really Harriet.

For this tortoise a gentle scratch makes a pretty good birthday gift.

It also took people a long time to realize that Harriet's hard shell has feelings. She spent many years giving rides to children. People painted on her shell. They even carved their names into it. She still has the scars. Today, Harriet has a much better life. She is well cared for and protected.

Unfortunately, her natural **habitat** is not as well protected. When people arrived they brought new animals to the islands, such as rats and goats. These animals compete for the same plants that the tortoises eat. The animals also eat tortoise eggs and babies. The good news is that laws now protect animals like Harriet. ■

Vocabulary

examine: to look at carefully, to study

habitat: the natural place where an animal lives

The World's Oldest

Animal	Name	Age	Place
goldfish	Tish	43	England
cat	Grandpa	34	Texas
Asian elephant	Lin Wang	86	China

Sequencing with Signal Words

Your Turn

Go back and write numbers next to events to put them in order. Look for signal words like *first*, *then*, *before*, and *finally*. Use that information to fill in the graphic organizer below.

Signal Words	Event 1

Signal Words	Events 2

Signal Words	Events 3

Signal Words	Events 4

Your Choice

Circle the correct answer.

1. **Harriet is —**

   A. the last tortoise on Galapagos.
   B. the oldest living tortoise.
   C. Charles Darwin's pet.
   D. the smallest living tortoise.

2. **Before Darwin visited the Galapagos Islands, —**

   A. giant tortoises were in danger of dying out.
   B. the Australia zoo asked him to find a tortoise for its collection.
   C. people did not know about the giant tortoises living there.
   D. Harriet was already 100 years old.

3. **After Harriet boarded the ship, she —**

   A. became the subject of a study by Charles Darwin.
   B. was born on the Galapagos Islands.
   C. was taken to a zoo in Australia.
   D. became famous.

4. **Harriet's natural habitat is —**

   A. an Australian zoo.
   B. on a boat.
   C. in England.
   D. the Galapagos Islands.

(See answers for Literal Skills, Lesson 9 to check your work.)

Number Correct:

Write Back...

How does putting events in order help you?

Lesson

10 Reading a Chart

Your Turn

Use the information in the chart to answer the questions below.

The World's Oldest			
Animal	**Name**	**Age**	**Place**
goldfish	Tish	43	England
cat	Grandpa	34	Texas
Asian elephant	Lin Wang	86	China

What animal on the chart is the oldest?

____

Where did the oldest cat live?

____

What is the name of the oldest goldfish?

____

Create a row on the chart for Harriet.

Animal	Name	Age	Place

Your Choice

Circle the correct answer.

1. **Today Harriet lives —**

   A. in the Pacific Ocean.
   B. on the Galapagos Islands.
   C. in Australia.
   D. in England.

2. **When compared with the other animals in the chart, Harriet —**

   A. is younger than Grandpa.
   B. is older than the other animals.
   C. isn't as old as Tish.
   D. is younger than Lin Wang.

3. **The chart tells you that the oldest goldfish is —**

   A. named Harriet.
   B. in England.
   C. 34 years old.
   D. unknown.

4. **Charles Darwin wanted to examine Harriet to —**

   A. learn about her.
   B. teach her tricks.
   C. help her grow.
   D. help her get well.

(See answers for Literal Skills, Lesson 10 to check your work.)

Number Correct:

Write Back...

How can charts help you organize information?

The Car/Boat

Is it a car? Is it a boat?

Comprehension Skills

- **Lesson 11:** Sequencing with Dates
- **Lesson 12:** Reading a Timeline

Reading Strategy

Retell

Check your understanding while reading. Cover up and retell parts of the passage. Then, uncover the part to see how well you did.

For many years people have wanted to build a car that can go on both land and water.

First Tries

The first try at building a car that could also be a boat was in 1899. Unfortunately, it didn't work. Then in 1942 a car and boat was built in the United States. It had a wooden covering and three wheels. The wheels pulled in when the car went into the water.

Over the years there have been other cars that could go on land and in water. For instance, the Raccoon was designed and built in France in 1993.

In September 2003, a better car and boat was built in England. This car drove off the road and into a river. It kept going—it worked! This car is called the Aquada. The Aquada is the best so far because it is fast and easily goes from land to water.

Not Easy

It took seventy **engineers** seven years to invent the Aquada. They began work in 1996. Sixty new ideas went into their invention. To make the Aquada work as a boat and a car, they had to solve many problems.

The Aquada can go 100 miles per hour on land. And it can go over 30 mph on water. That's fast!

This car and water truck went over land and water during World War II.

Making It Work

One problem was the propeller. A propeller goes around and around like a fan. It makes boats and other things move. A propeller does not work well for a car on land. So the Aquada uses an engine. On land, the engine turns the wheels as it does on other cars. In the water, a powerful jet pushes liquid and air out the back to move the Aquada along.

A second problem was that in water, wheels are not needed. They slow down the boat. When the Aquada goes into water, the driver presses a button. The wheels pull into the car's body and seem to disappear.

The third problem was the doors. Doors are great on land. But in water, they can leak. So there are no doors on the Aquada. It is open on top, and the driver and passengers climb into it.

Not to Worry

A fourth problem was that the car might turn into a boat on the highway. Don't worry. The Aquada has special **signals** that make that impossible!

All in all, the Aquada looks like a really fun ride! ■

The Long Road to Making a Car and Boat Together

- 1895
- 1899 First try at building a car and boat together.
- 1942 Car and boat built in the U.S.
- 1950
- 1993 The Racoon built in France.
- 1996 Work began on the Aquada.
- 2003 Aquada hits water.
- 2005

Vocabulary

engineers: people who use math and science to solve problems

signals: signs that give information

Lesson 11

Sequencing with Dates

Your Turn

Reread "The Car/Boat." Then, use dates to put events in order in the chart below.

Date	Event 1
Date	Event 2
Date	Event 3
Date	Event 4

Your Choice

Read the passage and circle the correct answer.

1. **The Aquada is the best boat and car so far because —**

   A. it had a propeller.
   B. it is fast and easy to use.
   C. it was made in England.
   D. it was built in France.

2. **When was a car and boat built that had a wooden covering?**

   A. In 1899
   B. In 2003
   C. After work began on the Aquada
   D. In 1942

3. **Pick the answer below that shows the correct time sequence.**

   A. Raccoon, then car and boat in U.S.
   B. first the Aquada, then the Raccoon
   C. first try, then car and boat built in U.S.
   D. Raccoon, then first try

4. **In paragraph 5, the word engineers means —**

   A. things that rotate.
   B. people who build cars.
   C. people who cause problems.
   D. people who solve problems.

(See answers for Literal Skills, Lesson 11 to check your work.)

Number Correct:

Write Back...

Think about a few important dates from your life. Write about what happened. Include the dates.

Reading a Timeline

Your Turn

Read the timeline and answer the questions.

The Long Road to Making a Car and Boat Together

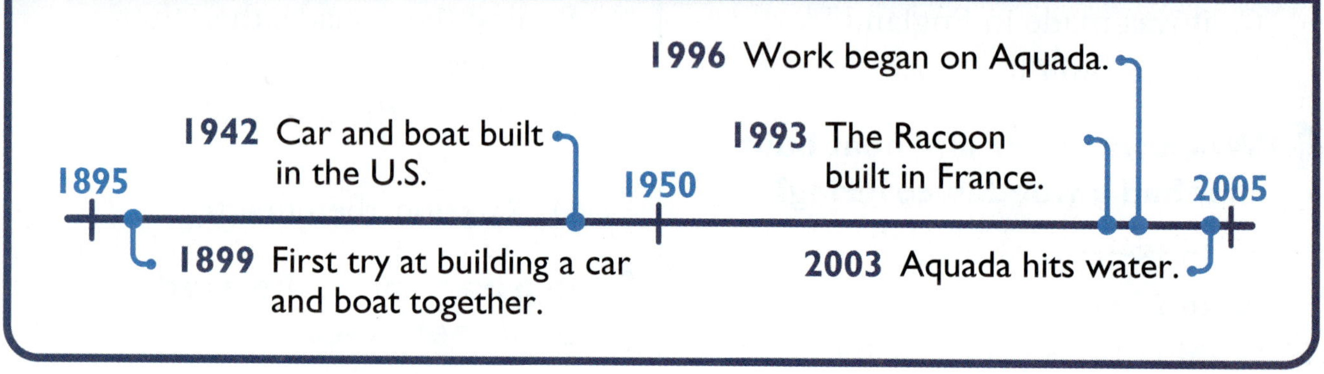

What is the title of the timeline?

What year was the Raccoon built?

How many years did it take to build the Aquada?

How many years passed between the first try at building a car and boat together and 2003?

Your Choice

Circle the correct answer.

1. **Which of these is not on the Aquada?**
   C. doors
   B. wheels
   A. buttons
   D. signals

2. **How many years passed between when work began on the Aquada and when it hit the water?**
   A. seven years
   B. one hundred years
   C. three years
   D. ten years

3. **On the timeline, which event happened in 1942?**
   A. The first try at building a car and boat was made.
   B. Work began on the Aquada.
   C. The Raccoon was built in France.
   D. A car and boat was built in the U.S.

4. **Signals on the Aquada are signs that —**
   A. do not give information.
   B. have ideas.
   C. warn of a problem.
   D. play music.

(See answers for Literal Skills, Lesson 12 to check your work.)

Number Correct:

Write Back...

Imagine you are retelling the passage to a friend. What would you include? What would you leave out? Why?

Fun, Playful, and Useless!

Who wants to toss around a two-foot long football?

Comprehension Skills

You Have Already Learned

- Sequencing with Signal Words
- Reading a Chart
- Sequencing with Dates
- Reading a Timeline

Most inventors make things that will be useful. Often it means making a better version of something. Some inventions are silly and should leave well enough alone!

A Better Football?

One inventor decided that a regular football is hard to throw. He thought a longer football would be better. By making it long and thin, a smaller hand could grip it. He came up with a football more than two feet long and **patented** this idea in 1985. Can you imagine how this design would change the game of football?

A Better Sleeping Bag

Another inventor did not want to climb out of a sleeping bag on a cold night. So he designed the walking sleeping bag. He put leg and arm holes in his sleeping bag. Straps hold

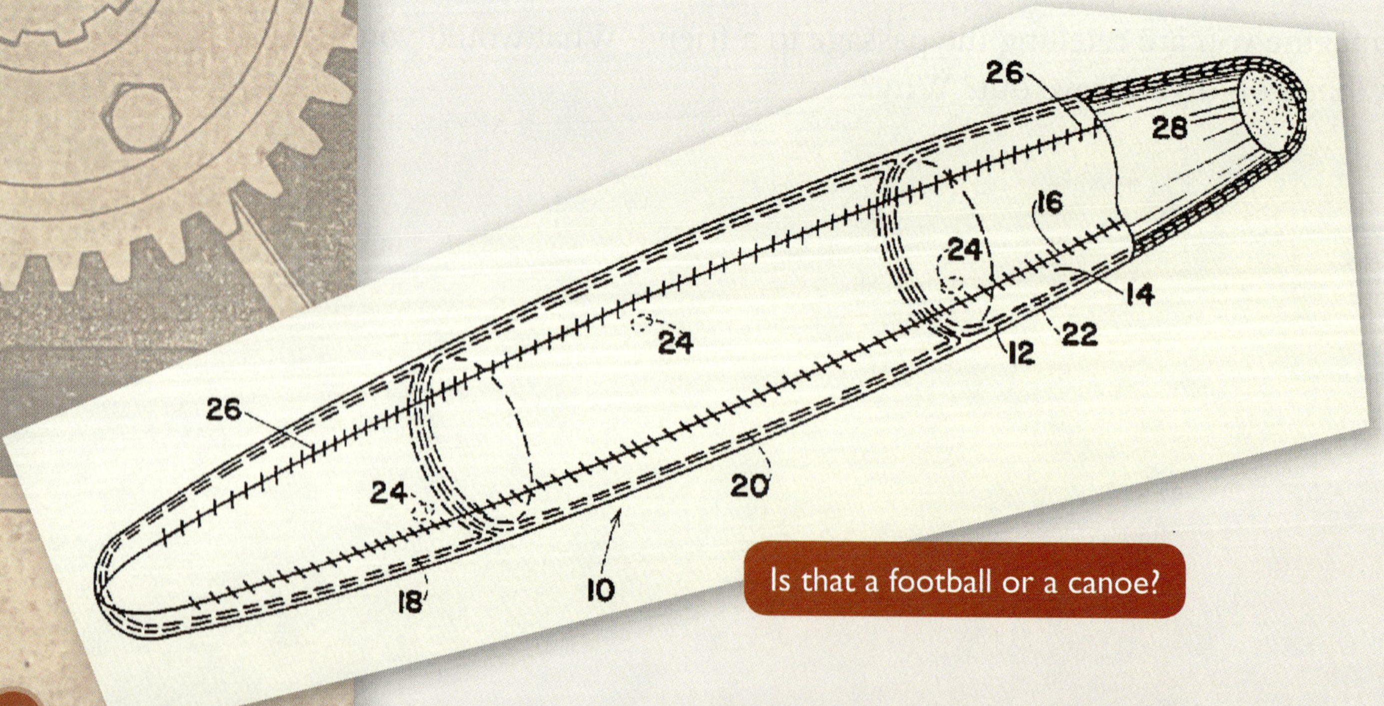

Is that a football or a canoe?

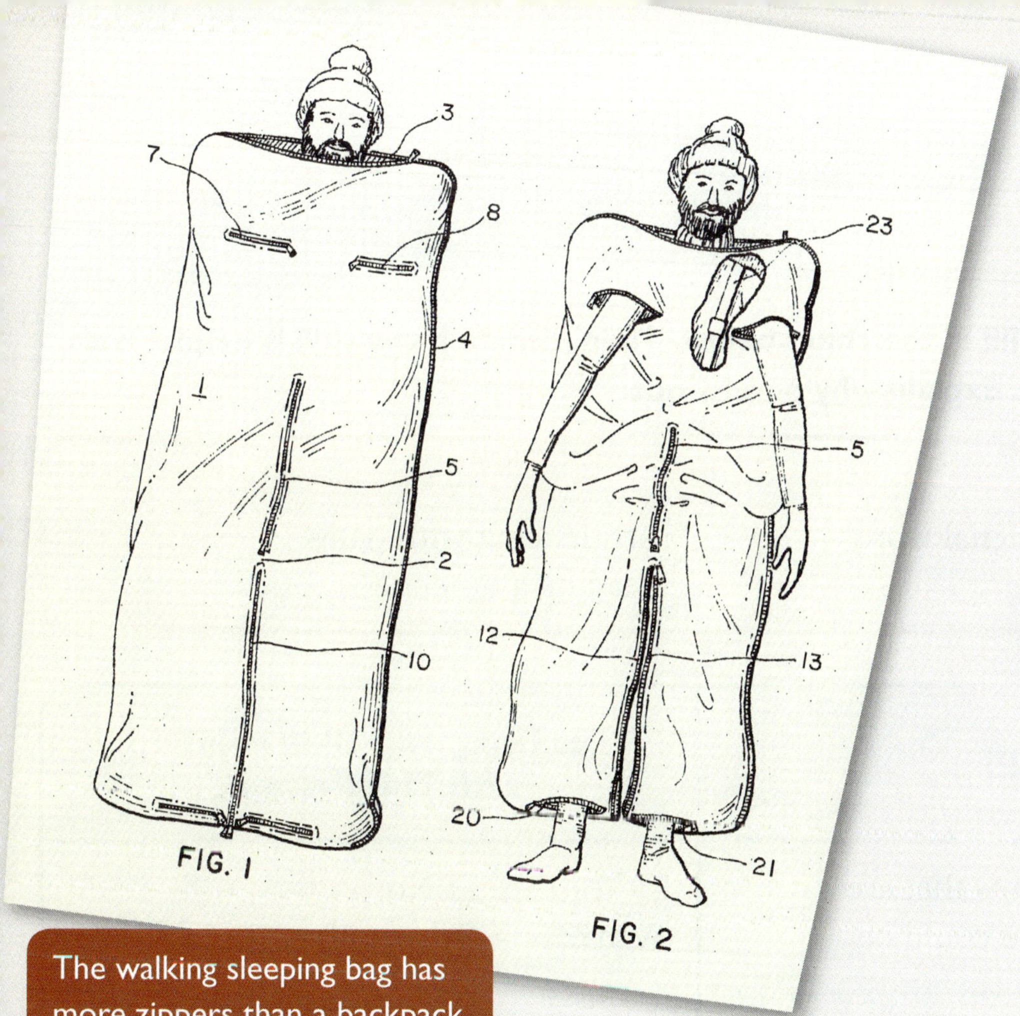

The walking sleeping bag has more zippers than a backpack.

the bag on. This allows the user to get up and walk around with the sleeping bag still in place. Now why would anyone go to all this trouble? Sleepwalkers?

An "ABC" Gum Locket

ABC (already been chewed) gum is not exactly a keepsake. Or is it? This jewelry item was patented in 1889. A space inside the locket hides your gum. It keeps the gum clean. Would you want to store old gum inside your jewelry? Most people would say no. That's something the inventor should have **considered.** ■

Vocabulary

patented: given the right to be made or sold

considered: thought carefully about something

Lesson 13 Review

Your Turn

Use the Skills List to fill in the chart below. Then, decide if the skill is helpful with what you are reading. Explain why or why not.

Skills List

- sequencing with signal words
- reading a chart
- sequencing with dates
- reading a timeline

Skill	Is Using This Skill Helpful with This Passage?
When you read events that are shown on a line, you could be ________________	☐ Yes Why? ☐ No Why not?
When you use signal words to recognize the sequence of events, you could be ________________	☐ Yes Why? ☐ No Why not?
When you use dates to recognize the sequence of events, you could be ________________	☐ Yes Why? ☐ No Why not?
When you read across columns and rows to get information, you could be ________________	☐ Yes Why? ☐ No Why not?

Your Choice

Circle the correct answer.

1 **The inventor of the longer football believes it —**

A. should be three feet long.
B. will bounce like any other.
C. is easier to grip.
D. is easier to kick.

2 **Which skill helps you tell which invention came first?**

A. reading a chart
B. sequencing with dates
C. reading a map
D. using titles and sidebars

3 **When was the chewing gum locket invented?**

A. around 1965.
B. around 1889.
C. after 1985.
D. before 1700.

4 **When you consider if something is useful, you —**

A. read all about it.
B. tell everyone about it.
C. write a letter about it.
D. think about it.

(See answers for Literal Skills, Lesson 13 to check your work.)

Number Correct:

Write Back...

Which literal skills are most useful with this passage?

Two World Records in One Balloon

Steve Fossett won a world record he wasn't trying to get.

Humans are always coming up with new **methods** of travel. One hundred years ago, it might have taken you four weeks to get some place. Today, however, that same trip is just a four hour flight. As long as you travel by jet, that is. After all, there is more than one way to fly. You could, for example, take a balloon.

Ever notice that there are no balloons at the airport? There is a good reason for this. Airplanes are faster than balloons. They can carry hundreds of people and are much easier to fly. Balloons, on the other hand, can get easily knocked off course. All it takes is one blast of wind in the wrong direction.

Comprehension Skills

- **Lesson 14:** Identifying Details on a Topic
- **Lesson 15:** Identifying Important and Unimportant Details

Reading Strategy

Retell

As you read, try to remember some facts. Then you can tell this story to someone else.

The balloon looks like it's made of aluminum foil. This helps keep the air hot at night when it gets really cold.

Steve Fossett flew a balloon non-stop around the world. And he set two world records doing it.

It's funny, when you stop to think about it. The year 1783 was the first time anyone flew in a hot-air balloon. Do you know what that means? People were flying around in balloons long before anyone even thought of an airplane.

The first airplane lifted off the ground in 1903. Twenty-one years later, in 1924, three planes flew all the way around the world. This flight was a world record in more ways than one. It took them 175 days.

Guess when the first hot-air balloon flew around the world. Go ahead, give it a guess. It was 1999. It took two guys twenty days. They flew 28,431 miles non-stop. For more than 200 years many **balloonists** had tried. No one was able to do it. That's how hard it is to fly around the world in a hot-air balloon.

In 2002, Steve Fossett circled the globe in a balloon. To set a new world record, he flew non-stop and alone. It took him 14 days, 19 hours, 50 minutes. High winds kept him from landing as soon as he wanted, so he also set the record for world's longest solo balloon flight. ■

FAST FACTS

1995—February 17–21
First solo crossing of the Pacific in a hot-air balloon.

1998—August 7–16
Longest distance ever flown solo in a hot-air balloon.

2002—June 19–July 2
Fastest flight around the world in a hot-air balloon.

2002—June 19–July 4
Longest solo balloon flight.

Vocabulary

method: a way of doing something

balloonists: people who fly balloons

Lesson 14

Identifying Details on a Topic

Your Turn

Asking yourself *who*, *what*, *when*, and *where* will help you find important details in "Two World Records in One Balloon."

Complete the graphic organizer.

Who

What

Topic

Two World Records in One Balloon

When

Where

Your Choice

Circle the correct answer.

1. **The first time anyone flew a hot air balloon was —**

   A. in 1999.
   B. in 2002.
   C. long after anyone flew an airplane.
   D. long before anyone flew an airplane.

2. **Knowing the *who*, *when*, and *where* of a story means you know —**

   A. how the story ends.
   B. three important story facts.
   C. how to read captions.
   D. what page you are on.

3. **If you want to know *why* the hot air balloon looks like it's made of aluminum foil, then you have to —**

   A. look at a map.
   B. read the caption.
   C. look at a timeline.
   D. give your own idea why.

4. **Which of the following is NOT a method of flying?**

   A. airplane
   B. balloon
   C. bicycle
   D. glider

(See answers for Literal Skills, Lesson 14 to check your work.)

Number Correct:

Write Back...

What did you learn about using the 4 *W*'s–*Who, What, When,* and *Where*? How does it help you to retell the story about Steve Fossett's balloon flight?

Lesson 15

Identifying Important and Unimportant Details

Your Turn

Important details are ones that have to do with the topic.

Reread "Two World Records in One Balloon." Find important and unimportant details. Write them into the boxes below.

Topic

Two World Records in One Balloon

Important Details	Unimportant Details

Your Choice

Circle the correct answer.

1. **Fossett set the world record for longest balloon flight alone when —**

   A. he asked to land at an airport.
   B. another balloon fell out of the race.
   C. he lost his map and couldn't find the finish line.
   D. high winds kept him from landing.

2. **Important details are —**

   A. any fact in a story.
   B. only in the captions.
   C. about the topic.
   D. missing facts.

3. **Which story detail is the most important?**

   A. There are no hot-air balloons at the airport.
   B. Fossett flew his balloon around the world in record time.
   C. High winds can knock a balloon off course.
   D. Airplanes first flew around the world in 1924.

4. **A balloonist would most likely know —**

   A. how to take a photograph from space.
   B. how to pull a balloon out of a hard wind.
   C. how to fix a flat tire.
   D. how to climb a mountain.

(See answers for Literal Skills, Lesson 15 to check your work.)

Number Correct:

Write Back...

How does knowing the topic help you tell what is important and unimportant in a story?

GET A GRIP!

What sport can send you up a wall?

These days anyone can be a rock climber, even if there's no mountain nearby. All you need is a gym with a climbing wall! It's not a mountain and it's not made of rock, but if you want to learn to climb, this is the place to go.

Climbing walls are mostly found in gyms, but some sporting goods stores have them too. You must pay to climb the walls in gyms. Often the walls in stores are free—at least for short periods of time. Both places show you how to climb, and they have people called spotters to keep you from falling when you are on the wall.

There are several major differences between going up a climbing wall and a mountain. Climbing walls are made to look rocky, but they have plastic handholds and footholds.

Comprehension Skills

- **Lesson 16:** Identifying a Stated Main Idea
- **Lesson 17:** Identifying Support for a Stated Main Idea

Reading Strategy

Reread

As you read, go back and reread. Sometimes it is easier to understand information the second time you read it.

Climbers develop strong arms, legs, and shoulders.

Spotters help, but climbers still need to watch what they're doing.

After several trips up the climbing wall you will learn where the handholds and footholds are. You can't do that on a mountain. On a mountain you have to search for a spot to hold onto every time. Also, outdoor rock climbers carve out handholds and footholds if they can't find one.

Climbing Safely

Wherever you climb, you'll need to be strapped into a safety **harness**. The harness fits over your body and is hooked to a rope. If you're indoors, the rope goes through a pulley at the top of the wall. The spotter on the ground holds the other end of the rope. This person keeps the rope at the right **tension**. If you need some slack in the rope to climb up higher, the spotter will loosen it a little. If you start to slip, the spotter will tighten the safety rope so you won't fall. So who needs a mountain when you can learn to climb a wall! ■

FUN FACT

Many walls have color-coded handholds and footholds. Beginning climbers follow one color. Other climbers follow the colors that mark harder paths up the wall.

Vocabulary

harness: straps that help keep the body in control

tension: how loose or tight something is

Lesson 16

Identifying a Stated Main Idea

Your Turn

Use clues from your reading to find a stated main idea. Read the title and any headings. They will give you clues. Then, look in the first and last paragraphs for a sentence that sums up what the reading is about.

Title

Headings

The first paragraph is about

The last sentence says

A sentence that sums up what this reading is all about

Your Choice

Circle the correct answer.

1. **Climbing walls can be found in —**

   A. handholds and footholds.
   B. rocks and mountains.
   C. gyms and stores.
   D. colors and patterns.

2. **The main idea of the first paragraph is —**

   A. you must keep safe.
   B. anyone can be a rock climber.
   C. you can climb in a store.
   D. you can climb with a spotter.

3. **Paragraph four is about —**

   A. how to climb safely.
   B. a way to push your feet.
   C. a way to place your hands.
   D. how to hold the rope.

4. **If the rope has too much tension, the —**

   A. spotter must be on a mountain.
   B. spotter is holding it very tight.
   C. rope is not attached to the wall.
   D. handholds and footholds are in the wrong place.

(See answers for Literal Skills, Lesson 16 to check your work.)

Number Correct:

Write Back...

How can knowing the main idea is help you understand what you read?

Lesson

17 Identifying Support for a Stated Main Idea

Your Turn

If you have found the main idea, finding support for it should be easy. The rest of the text should support this main idea. If you're having trouble, check out whether or not you have the right main idea.

Remember to use these clues to find the main idea.

- look at the title and the headings
- read the first paragraph
- read the last paragraph

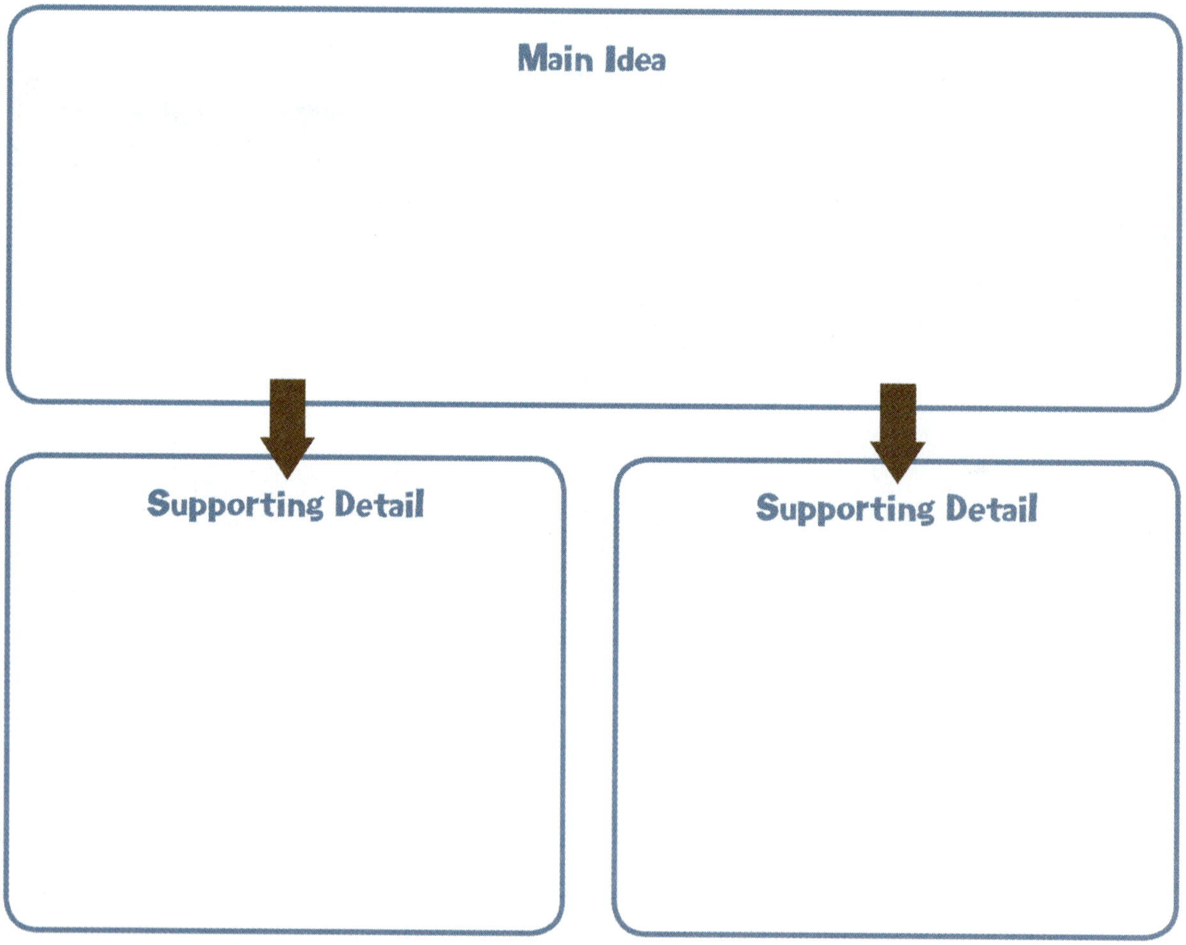

Your Choice

Circle the correct answer.

1. **The difference between walls in a gym and walls in a sporting goods store is —**

   A. you have to pay in gyms.
   B. they are both for beginners.
   C. both have plastic handholds.
   D. spotters help out in gyms.

2. **Which sentence gives a detail about climbing safely?**

   A. You can crawl up a climbing wall!
   B. The rope goes through a pulley at the top of the wall.
   C. All climbing walls are big.
   D. Now there are no excuses.

3. **Which paragraph tells about the difference between walls and mountains?**

   A. the first
   B. the third
   C. the second
   D. the fourth

4. **Without a harness, climbers —**

   A. wouldn't have to pay.
   B. could go much higher.
   C. would need more spotters.
   D. could fall and get hurt.

(See answers for Literal Skills, Lesson 17 to check your work.)

Number Correct:

Write Back...

Why is it helpful to find support for the main idea?

REUSE THOSE TAPES

What business gets paid to erase?

Comprehension Skills

You Have Already Learned

- Using Text Features
- Scanning for Keywords
- Using Parts of a Book
- Reading a Map, Timeline, or Chart
- Understanding Directions
- Sequencing with Signal Words
- Sequencing with Dates
- Identifying Details on a Topic
- Identifying Important and Unimportant Details
- Identifying a Stated Main Idea
- Identifying Support for a Main Idea

What do TV stations do with old tapes? They used to throw them away. Sometimes they destroyed them. David Paul Cohen thought that was a waste. He decided he could make money from those tapes.

A Plan for Business

In 1993, David Cohen made a plan. He set up a business in his garage. His company would recycle old tapes. First he had to clean the tapes. Then, he erased them. After that, he was able to sell them again.

An Idea for Customers

Customers like the idea. They could buy good used tapes for $7.00. New tapes cost over $13.00. Customers found that the used tapes were just as good as new ones. Cohen's tapes sold fast!

David Cohen's company is one of the country's 500 fastest-growing companies.

David's company is all about recycling. He makes money by reusing old tapes.

Cohen knew that TV and movie companies liked the idea of recycling, too. Destroying tapes took a lot of time and money. And no one likes more trash filling up landfills. Tapes are even worse than most trash because they don't **decompose** easily. They stay in landfills for a long time.

So Cohen asked TV and movie companies to mail their old tapes to him. The companies were happy to recycle. They knew Cohen would make good use of the tapes.

A Good Place to Work

People like working for Cohen. Cohen pays his workers well. He gives them extra benefits like time to play games. He cares about workers' families.

Cohen also cares about people who don't work for him. His company gives money to help people in need.

In 2000, Cohen's workers wrote a letter to the government. They suggested that Cohen win the United States Young **Entrepreneur** of the Year Award. The government agreed. David Paul Cohen is a great young entrepreneur.

Vocabulary

decompose: to break down
entrepreneur: a person who starts a business

Lesson 18

Review

Your Turn

Use the Skills List to fill in the chart below. Then, decide if the skill is helpful with what you are reading. Explain why or why not.

Skills List

- using text features
- scanning for keywords
- using parts of a book
- reading a map, timeline, or chart
- understanding directions
- sequencing with signal words
- sequencing with dates
- identifying details on a topic
- identifying important and unimportant details
- identifying a stated main idea
- identifying support for a main idea

Skill	Is Using This Skill Helpful with This Passage?
When you find parts of a passage that explain a main idea, you could be ________________	☐ Yes Why? ☐ No Why not?
When you find important words about the topic, you could be ________________	☐ Yes Why? ☐ No Why not?
When you find the sentence that tells the most important idea in a passage, you could be ________________	☐ Yes Why? ☐ No Why not?
When you decide which information matters and which doesn't, you could be ________________	☐ Yes Why? ☐ No Why not?

Your Choice

Circle the correct answer.

1. **People liked to work for David because —**

   A. he gave them time to play games.
   B. he paid them with recycled tapes.
   C. he gave them tapes.
   D. their work was easy.

2. **What is the stated main idea of "Reuse Those Tapes"?**

   A. He decided he could make money from those old tapes.
   B. Cohen's tapes sold fast.
   C. David Paul Cohen is a great young entrepreneur.
   D. Cohen recycled the tapes and sold them.

3. **What does David Cohen's company have to do first?**

   A. sell tapes
   B. erase tapes
   C. clean tapes
   D. get old tapes

4. **David became an entrepreneur when he —**

   A. gave money to people.
   B. worked for a TV company.
   C. opened a business.
   D. won an award.

(See answers for Literal Skills, Lesson 18 to check your work.)

Number Correct:

Write Back...

Which skill helped you most as you read "Reuse Those Tapes"? Explain why.

Independent Reading Record

Use the graphic organizers from pages 63–79 to practice these Literal skills with the other books you read.

Skill	Title of Book and Pages
Using Text Features: Titles and Sidebars	
Using Text Features: Images and Captions	
Scanning for Keywords	
Using Parts of a Book	
Reading a Map	
Understanding Directions	
Sequencing with Signal Words	
Reading a Chart	
Sequencing with Dates	
Reading a Timeline	
Identifying Details on a Topic	
Identifying Important and Unimportant Details	
Identifying a Stated Main Idea	
Identifying Support for a Stated Main Idea	
Review Literal Skills	

Lesson 2

Using Text Features: Titles and Sidebars

Read the title, the headings in the text, and the sidebar headings. Then, fill in the boxes below.

The title tells me that this passage is about —

One of the sections of the passage is about —

Another section of the passage is about —

The sidebar is about —

Lesson 3

Using Text Features: Images and Captions

Look at the images, or pictures. Read the captions. Then, fill in the boxes below.

One picture shows —	Its caption tells about —

Another picture shows —	Its caption tells about —

Lesson 4

Scanning for Keywords

Keywords are words that are important to a topic. They can help you understand what you read.

Write the topic in the middle. Ask for help if you don't know the topic. Scan the passage for keywords. Write them around the topic.

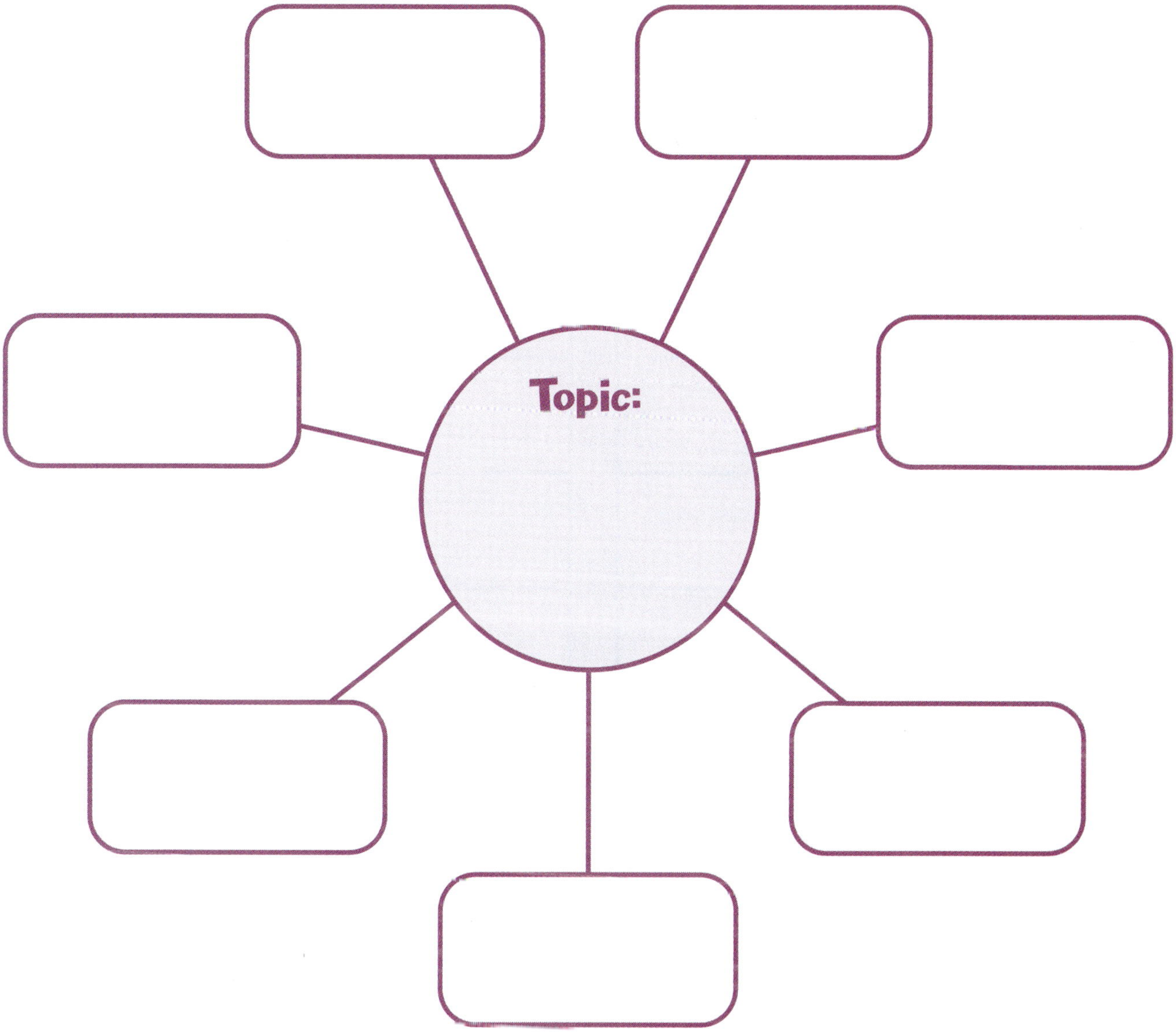

Lesson 5 Using Parts of a Book

Many books have a glossary and an index in the back. These are good study tools.

Use a glossary to learn the meaning of words.

When you read a word that you do not know, write it in the Word box below. Then, find the word in the glossary and write its meaning under Definition.

Use an index for topics you want to learn more about.

If there is a topic that interests you, write it in the Topic box below. Then find it in the index and write the page numbers. This tells you where to go in your book to find out more.

Glossary	
Word	Definition

Index	
Topic	Page

Lesson 6

Reading a Map

Fill out this checklist when you read a map.

Map of

____

The **title** on a map tells what information the map is meant to give.

The title on my map tells me that it is about

____.

The **compass rose** on a map shows the directions. It points to the north, south, east, and west.

On my map, ________________ is north of ________________

and ________________ is west of ________________.

The **scale** on a map shows the distance from one place to another. You can use it as a ruler.

On my map, the distance between ________________

and ________________ is ________________.

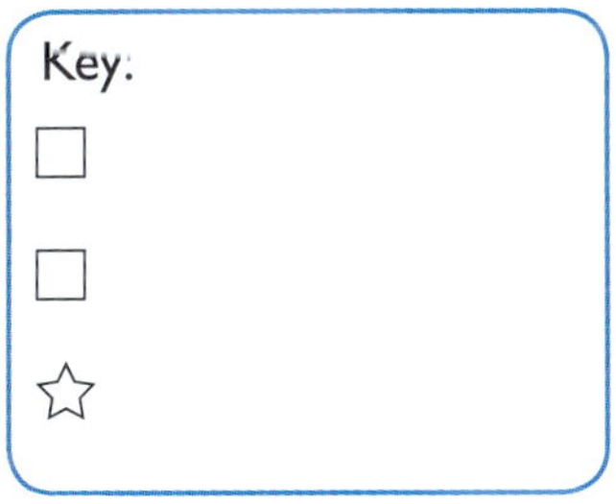

The **key** on a map shows what different colors and symbols mean.

On my map, ______________________________

means ______________________________________.

Lesson 7

Understanding Directions

Write each step for completing a task in the chart below. Be sure to put them in order.

How to ______________________________

Step 1

↓

Step 2

↓

Step 3

↓

Step 4

↓

Step 5

Lesson 8

Review

Use the Skills List to fill in the chart. Then, decide if the skill is helpful with what you are reading. Explain why or why not.

Skills List

- reading a map
- scanning for keywords
- using parts of a book
- understanding directions
- using text features: titles and sidebars
- using text features: images and captions

Skill	Is Using This Skill Helpful with This Passage?
When you read the title and headings to get the gist of a passage, you could be ________________	☐ Yes Why? ☐ No Why not?
When you carefully read instructions on how to do something, you could be ________________	☐ Yes Why? ☐ No Why not?
When you use a scale, compass rose, and key to study a map, you could be ________________	☐ Yes Why? ☐ No Why not?
When you learn about a passage by looking at pictures, you could be ________________	☐ Yes Why? ☐ No Why not?
When you look quickly for important words, you could be ________________	☐ Yes Why? ☐ No Why not?
When you use a book's index to find information, you could be ________________	☐ Yes Why? ☐ No Why not?

Lesson 9

Sequencing with Signal Words

Look for signal words such as *first*, *next*, *then*, and *finally*. Fill in this chart with events in the correct order. You may add boxes or cross out the ones you don't need.

Signal Words	Event 1

Signal Words	Event 2

Signal Words	Event 3

Signal Words	Event 4

Lesson 10

Reading a Chart

Use this checklist when you come across a chart in your reading.

- ☐ Check the chart's title. What does it tell you about the information in the chart?

- ☐ Check the heading of each column. What does the heading tell you about the information in each column?

- ☐ Check each row. What kinds of examples are in each row?

- ☐ Check for what can be compared. How can you compare information in the chart?

Lesson 11

Sequencing with Dates

You can often figure out the sequence, or order, of events by looking at dates.

Write one event in each of the boxes in the time order of how it occurred. Then, write the date that was used to signal time.

Date	Event 1

Date	Event 2

Date	Event 3

Date	Event 4

Lesson 12

Reading a Timeline

Use the checklist below as you read a timeline.

The title on a timeline tells what information the timeline is meant to give.

The title on my timeline tells me that it is about

____.

A horizontal timeline shows events from left to right. The items on the left happened first. The items on the right are the most recent.

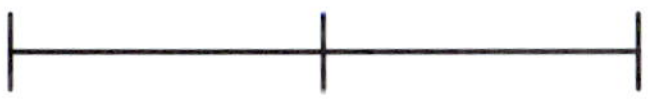

On my timeline, ____________________ happend first in __________. ____________________ happened last in __________.

A vertical timeline shows events from top to bottom. The items on the top happened first. The items on the bottom are the most recent.

On my timeline, ____________________ happend first in __________. ____________________ happened last in __________.

On most horizontal timelines, the date appears above each event point. The description of the event appears below.

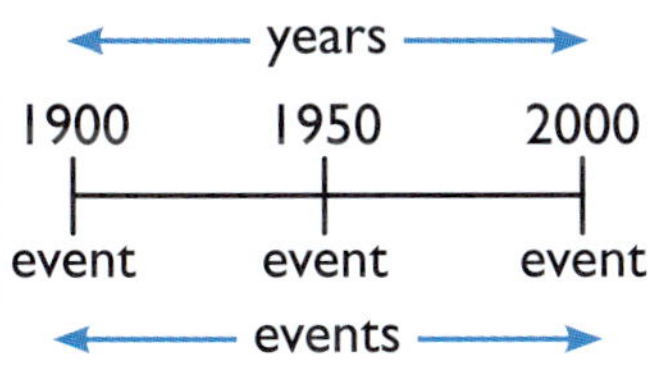

The first event on my timeline happend in __________.

It is described as ________________________________.

Lesson 13
Review

Use the Skills List to fill in the chart. Then, decide if the skill is helpful with what you are reading. Explain why or why not.

Skills List
- sequencing with signal words
- reading a chart
- sequencing with dates
- reading a timeline

Skill	Is Using This Skill Helpful with This Passage?
When you use clue words to understand the order of events, you could be ______	☐ Yes Why? ☐ No Why not?
When you read events on a line to see the order and time that they happened, you could be ______	☐ Yes Why? ☐ No Why not?
When you look at columns and rows to find information, you could be ______	☐ Yes Why? ☐ No Why not?
When you look at dates in a passage to determine the order things happened, you could be ______	☐ Yes Why? ☐ No Why not?

Lesson 14

Identifying Details on a Topic

Fill in each box with details from the story. Ask for help if you do not know the topic.

Who

What

Topic

When

Where

Lesson

15 Identifying Important and Unimportant Details

Write the topic into the box at the top. Ask for help if you do not know the topic. Then, write important and important details into each box.

Topic	
Important Details	**Unimportant Details**

Lesson 16

Identifying a Stated Main Idea

Use clues from your reading to find a stated main idea. Read the title and any headings. They will give you clues. Then, look in the first and last paragraphs for a sentence that sums up what the reading is about.

Title

Headings or Chapter Titles

The first paragraph is about

The last sentence says

A sentence that sums up what this reading is all about

Lesson 17

Identifying Support for a Stated Main Idea

If you have found the main idea, finding support for it should be easy. The rest of the text should support this main idea. If you're having trouble, check out whether or not you have the right main idea.

Remember to use clues to find the main idea.
- look at the title, headings, and chapter titles
- read the first paragraph
- read the last paragraph

Main Idea

Supporting Detail

Supporting Detail

Review

Use the Skills List to fill in the chart. Then, decide if the skill is helpful with what you are reading. Explain why or why not.

Skills List

- using text features
- scanning for keywords
- using parts of a book
- reading a map, timeline, or chart
- understanding directions
- sequencing with signal words
- sequencing with dates
- identifying details on a topic
- identifying important and unimportant details
- identifying a stated main idea
- identifying support for a main idea

Skill	Is Using This Skill Helpful with This Passage?
When you find the most important idea written in a passage, you could be ____________	☐ Yes Why? ☐ No Why not?
When you read titles, headings, and captions to get the gist of a passage, you could be ____________	☐ Yes Why? ☐ No Why not?
When you use dates or clue words to determine which events happen first, you could be ____________	☐ Yes Why? ☐ No Why not?
When you decide which information matters and what doesn't, you could be ____________	☐ Yes Why? ☐ No Why not?
When you use a table of contents, or index to find information, you could be ____________	☐ Yes Why? ☐ No Why not?